BLUFF YOUR WAY IN MATH

Robert Ainsley

CENTENNIAL PRESS

ISBN 0-8220-2214-1
U.S. edition Copyright © 1990 by Centennial Press
British edition Copyright © 1988 by The Bluffer's Guides

Printed in U.S.A.

Centennial Press, Box 82087, Lincoln, Nebraska 68501
an imprint of Cliffs Notes, Inc.

WHAT IS MATHEMATICS?

The word *mathematics* comes from a Greek word meaning *learning*, which might seem peculiar, since mathematicians are usually anything but learned and the deepest literature most of them try is *The Hitch Hiker's Guide to the Galaxy*. But mathematics was no doubt thus named for the same reason the Vikings called the newly discovered island they wanted to populate quickly Greenland—instead of Icy Cold Miserable Barren Glacier-Ridden Land. If you want to make a subject seem interesting, you've got to jazz up the title a little and make the thing sound impressive. So the bluffer should always insist on the full title *mathematics*—and scorn the more casual term *math*. ("A math," you should say caustically, "ith a Roman Catholic thervithe.")

Mathematics is in a funny position—not really accessible enough to be an art and not immediately useful enough to be a science. It's generally hard to understand, contradicts common sense much of the time, and is Public Enemy No. 1 of the academic disciplines.

It's so rare to find someone who's good at mathematics that employers often require college-level proficiency strictly as a convenient way to cut down the deluge of applicants for their opening for janitor, or bus driver, or Chairman of the Federal Reserve, or any of the other jobs traditionally handled by people who can't add two and two. Knowing your way around the convolutions of mathematics will get you instant respect; mathematicians, the uninitiated believe, have the ability to think when they're faced with a problem. And to some extent, it's true—most mathematicians can barely take out their garbage, and with anything more complicated, all they *can* do is think about it. By bluffing your way in mathematics and thereby creating the impression of having an analytical, logical, and clear-thinking brain, you'll leave them standing open-mouthed eating your dust.

The Basics

There are lots of books about mathematics—usually excruciatingly long ones with thousands of pages of tiny print without pictures, full of strings of odd-looking, apparently meaningless characters—like any university mathematics faculty. We can, however, describe the function of mathematics quite simply. Mathematics consists essentially of

(1) proving the obvious,
(2) proving the not so obvious, and
(3) proving the obviously false to be true.

Mathematicians are allowed to create tortuous complexity in illustrating what everyone already knows. For example, it took mathematicians until the 1800s to prove that $1+1=2$, and not before the late 1970s were they confident of proving that any map requires no more than four colors to make it look good, a fact known by cartographers for centuries.

There are many not-so-obvious things which can be

proved to be true too or too true. Like the fact that for any group of 23 people, there's an even chance two or more of them share a birthday. (With groups of twins, this becomes almost certain. Not *quite* certain, as you'll of course point out; they might have all been born on the opposite sides of midnight.)

Mathematicians are also fond of proving things which are obviously false, like all straight lines being curved and a busy telephone being just as likely to be free if you call again immediately as it would if you wait 20 minutes. They also like disproving things which are obviously true — for example, that the shortest distance between two points on the earth's surface on an airline route always goes across Anchorage, Alaska.

Convincing people that you know the esoterica of mathematics will leave them with deep-seated insecurities and you with a psychological hand full of trump cards. To normal people, it's a mysterious, bewildering world, a system they remember vaguely from their school days — jumbled memories of chanting multiplication tables and problems about two trains traveling at different speeds to Sheboygan — apparently designed specifically to confuse them (it was). Why, they ask, do mathematicians talk about x's and y's? Why don't they call a spade a spade? Well, you can say, spades are not *always* spades. Sometimes spades are trumps. And most card tricks are just simple exercises in mathematics anyway.

It's important to be supportive when you're talking mathematics; nod sympathetically and reassure them that it's just "badly taught," that schools lack the money and resources to "make the subject come alive" and don't know how to make mathematics fun, "which, of course, it can and should be." Complete garbage, of course. Mathematics is deadly boring, as everyone knows—otherwise there wouldn't be so many books with earnest and well-meaning titles like *Matrices Can Be Fun* and *Calculus Made Easy*, which have really inspiring things on the cover like tetrahedrons with *x* written on them. You've got to imply that it's an intellectual laugh a minute if you're bright enough to appreciate it.

However, you don't ever have to try to justify the existence of mathematics, let alone the existence of outdated school courses and textbooks with titles like *Essential Modern Math*, which are always full of completely unnecessary and old-fashioned things like Venn diagrams. Mathematics is its own justification; to those who question its relevance or application, assume an imperious tone and make up some spiel about what a really interesting and important thing it is. Employ at random in your reply phrases like the "purity of mathematics," "mathematics as a tool," "intrinsic patterns," "a bridge between arts and science," "training of the mind in logical thinking," etc. If some miserable quibbler asks you a tedious question, such as what the Lax-Wendroff theorem is for, slap him down with "For? What do you mean, what's it for? It's not *for* anything. It's the *truth*." Don't fall into the trap many mathematicians set for themselves when, unable to shut up once they've won, they continue with something like "You might as well ask what a Beethoven symphony is for." The snappy comeback this will produce is that anyone can listen to and appreciate a Beethoven symphony, but only a few hundred people in the world can understand the Lax-Wendroff theorem (and very few of them could tell you what it *is* for).

Mathematics still strikes terror in the hearts of all normal, sane people, and anybody who professes to understand *any* of it will instantly skyrocket in the estimation of nonbluffers. Your chances of being challenged by someone who actually knows what they're talking about are one in a million, or as the mathematician would say, almost certainly totally improbable.

Arithmetic

There are great advantages to being a mathematician:

(1) You don't have to be able to spell.
(2) You don't have to be able to add.
(3) You don't have to be able to write legibly.

The illiteracy of mathematicians is a given. Mathematics educators, for example, are convinced that "arithmetic" begins with *r*, as do "riting" and "reading" (the nearest most mathematicians get to reading is on the freeway).

The myth still persists that mathematics somehow involves numbers. People fondly believe that mathematics majors spend their time doing long division by 173 and learning their 39's multiplication table. In fact, the reverse is true. Mathematicians are renowned for their inability to add or subtract, in much the same way as geographers are always getting lost and economists are always borrowing money off you. Never play Monopoly with a mathematician, or at least, don't let him be the banker.

You can, of course, work this to your advantage; when the accuracy of your arithmetic is questioned, say with indignation, "Of course I can't add; I'm a mathematician."

Most of mathematics is, in fact, devoted to avoiding arithmetic. The amount of adding, dividing, and subtracting decreases logarithmically as you progress through your mathematics career, and the numbers you'll encounter disappear accordingly. Elementary school kids can count to a million. High school kids have already started replacing numbers by x and y, but they only use numbers up to a hundred. College students handle numerals up to ten, but they've substituted letters for most numbers so persistently that they've run out of Roman letters and have to use Greek letters like π and α. In grad school, the only numbers you'll ever see are 0, 1, and 8, except that it's written on its side, pronounced "infinity," and means "lots." By this time, all the letters of the alphabet have long since been used up, the Greek alphabet is just about done for, and people working in set theory have to start on the Hebrew alphabet and use **alephs** and **gimuls.**

The bluffer should mention in passing here that the Russians and Chinese use x's, y's, a's, b's, c's, and so forth in their mathematical expositions. This kind of comment strongly suggests (without your direct confirmation) that you're multilingual and casually browse through the *Moscow Math Quarterly* and the *People's Mathematical Daily* in their native languages.

Nonmathematicians stand out like Captain Ahab at a save-the-whales rally when they try to use unknowns in propositions because they're too obvious — "Suppose

I earn x number of dollars a week," they say. A skilled bluffer sounds infinitely more sophisticated; he or she knows the Greek letters, the Cyrillic alphabet, and odd smidgens of Hebrew script and sneaks them in whenever possible. Make Greek symbols, in particular, second nature in your conversations. Use exotic letters, subscripts if possible, **theta-one** and **omega-zero,** for example: "If I earn Θ_1 dollars per week . . .," "Let's say our company produces Ω_0 units this year . . .," etc. You'll get good value for your verbal buck by using parentheses to indicate that one quantity is somehow dependent on the other, as in "Now suppose our productivity as a function of time is P_β *(t)* . . ." It'll net you instant adulation. The strategy has an added advantage — you don't have to have a clue as to what you're talking about; no one will dare argue with someone so eloquent and logically incisive. Some mathematicians insist on using the letter n to means "lots of," as in "I drank n fuzzy navels last night," in a feeble attempt at humor. Avoid this letter.

Except for the broad generalities we've given you, you don't really need to be concerned about "what mathematics is." It's a whole lot more productive to wait for someone else to talk about it, immediately pounce on them, and imply that they have a vastly more inferior grasp of things than you do, that they have some howler of a misconception that's so elementary that you can't begin to explain it. If they've made a genuine mistake or used a term loosely, don't give them an inch of slack to wiggle out of it. Some are obvious; when, for example, a loquacious football color commentator gushes that the team gave a 110 percent today, smile knowingly and chuckle quietly to yourself. When he says it's still mathematically possible for them to win the championship, mutter, "You mean *arithmetically* possible." When he says the chances of today's turn of events being repeated are a million to one, you say, "A million to one *against*, presumably."

Logic is the cornerstone of mathematics, and you can often catch people in the sloppy use of logic, especially when they play fast and loose with the syllogism. Here's a good example of syllogistic chaos:

Things that are good for you taste lousy.
This tastes lousy.
Therefore, this must be good for you.

Point out acidly that the conclusion doesn't follow at all, any more than this one works:

Carrots can't drive tractors.
The Empire State Building can't drive a tractor.
Therefore, the Empire State Building is a carrot.

In the study of formal logic, it's possible to start from nothing at all but, by proceeding purely logically, show that everything is true. The most important rule of logical inference like this is called **modus ponens.** Using this rule, you can, for example, infer from the statements

(1) If my aunt had male hormones she'd be my uncle.

and

(2) According to the tests, my aunt has male chromosomes.

the logical conclusion that

(3) Therefore, my aunt is my uncle.

Mathematics is a very exact science and must be very rigorously applied.

As an illustration of the kind of nitpicking that's essential to a mathematician — or anybody who wants to masquerade as one — it's useful to recall the story of the engineer, the physicist, and the mathematician at a conference together in China. Out on a day trip, the engineer spots a black pig in a field. "Look!" he exclaims, "pigs in China are black!"

"No," corrects the physicist, "you mean there's at least one pig in China that's black."

"Not quite," says the mathematician. "You mean there's at least one pig in China that's at least half black."

Even if you can't identify a mistake like this one, challenge any statement that's even vaguely mathematical. In order to defend your credibility as a mathematical savant, the best defense is immediate, seemingly sure-footed attack. And if you can't come up with a genuine criticism, general comments like the following will cover your posterior in most situations just fine. They'll make your conversational pigeon retire to his snug little nest to cogitate on your superior understanding of the situation (however misguided it may actually be). You can use these gems of misdirection in almost any situation, preceded, of course, by a thoughtful pause and eventual head nodding.

- Well, in this case, yes . . .
- Mmmm, yes, as long as the temperature/money supply/chance of precipitation/rate of inflation (use anything, the more irrelevant the better) stays constant.
- On a basic level, sure, I suppose you could say that.

11

If, in some perverse, knee-jerk rush of sympathy, you want to agree wholeheartedly with someone's proposition, at least imply some higher level of intuition, as in

- Yes . . . in fact, that holds for all similar cases, doesn't it?

Always question figures. You can trip up anyone on anything if they try to bury you in figures. Use one of these:

- I guess the figures are interesting—but they don't really tell you anything, do they?
- They seem a little rough—too rough, if you ask me.
- They seem fairly accurate—suspiciously accurate, if you ask me.

If, on the other hand, someone has the temerity to challenge *your* figures, say, "It's obvious," and stare at them bug-eyed in disbelief, as though you can't imagine how anyone but Zsa Zsa Gabor could possibly fail to understand your viewpoint.

MATHEMATICS SUPERSTARS

Since mathematics is generally either right or wrong, its superstars are above criticism because all the work they produced was right (well, almost all of it, anyway). So you can't really classify them into good and bad or ones you like and ones you don't as you would with composers, although you can often score points by demonstrating your knowledge of their private lives. Knowing that Newton died a virgin will get you more attention, and probably more action, at most parties than being able to prove the binomial theorem.

As a savvy bluffer, you'll always have some big names ready to drop into any conversation, and you'll be conversant with the work of the greats, in name at least. No one will ever have the confidence to challenge you to prove Leibniz's theorem or to integrate sine x; the names are always enough.

The Babylonians

They invented time, which the Egyptians never had the time to do. Because they counted up to 59 in the normal way but then, for some inexplicable reason, counted in units of 60 from there on, the world has had 60 seconds in a minute and 60 minutes in an hour ever since. For similar reasons linked to astronomy, there are 360 degrees in a circle and 360 days in a year, plus five and a fraction. The Babylonians knew about Pythagoras's theorem in a rough-and-ready kind of way, but they never realized its potential to terrorize school children and neglected to follow up on it.

Thales (*fl.* 585 B.C.)

The first mathematician who would admit to being one. He invented proofs and a smattering of geometry, and on discovering his fourth proposition (that a triangle drawn in a semicircle is always a right triangle), was so pleased that he went out and made a sacrifice to the gods: a bull. Geometry has appeared that way to many people ever since.

Pythagoras (*fl.* 530 B.C.)

The second mathematician. Popularizer of the right triangle and the first person to breed a hypotenuse in captivity. Pythagoras was famous for scratching out diagrams in the sand. It was here that he discovered the world's first theorem—that the square of the hypotenuse is equal to the sum of the squares of the other two sides. He met his end when he told a Roman soldier to stop walking over his hypotenuses and the soldier, who decided he couldn't stand a smartass, killed him. This was rather a shame because Pythagoras led his own commune, who sat around in the sun all day drinking and talking about infinity, and seems to have been been quite a hippie.

The Romans were not much good at mathematics.

They used Roman numerals to perform calculations and had a patently ridiculous way of handling fractions. Their system of writing mathematics was even more cumbersome than the Greeks', who just wrote everything out longhand. The Romans were much more concerned with building central-heating systems and viaducts and earning money than sitting around in the sun all day talking about infinity. They set the pattern for engineers to come.

There are, of course, several hundred ways of proving the **Pythagorean theorem,** so if you have to bluff your way through a proof of it, almost anything will do. Scratch a few plausible-looking triangles and squares in the sand or on the dashboard or on the restaurant tablecloth, keep mentioning the words "hypotenuse," "area," and "square," and make sure that at the most obscure and incomprehensible step in the proof, you use the mathematician's trick of saying, "Now here's the slick part."

Euclid (*fl.* 350 B.C.)

Produced a definitive work on all geometry in a series of books called *Elements*. In this, Euclid designed the first straight lines, points, and plane – the **Euclidean plane.** Sadly, on its maiden flight, it flew too close to the sun and its wings melted.

In the final book of this huge work, he introduced the **Platonic solids.** Most solid shapes before Plato (eggs, balls, lumps of Play-Doh, etc.) had been used by the Greeks for a variety of unsavory activities, but he put a stop to it by inventing this new set of objects to be used platonically. These are geometric shapes made out of polystyrene, which occur naturally in take-out restaurants. They're all perfectly regular and have a number of faces, like a good politician (politics was also, of course, invented in Greece). There are only five known to man – the four-sided **tetrahedron** (common), the six-sided **hexahedron**, or cube (common), the eight-sided **octahedron** (rare), a thing with twelve sides (**dodecahedron** – very rare), and a twenty-sided thing (the **icosahedron**, which doesn't occur outside Trivial Pursuit). The wise bluffer will, of course, know these names by heart. Faced with the difficulty of finding a name for an object with more than twenty sides, Plato desisted from designing any more.

Archimedes (287–212 B.C.)

The greatest of the Greek mathematicians, Archimedes sprang to fame when he ran naked through the streets of Greece shouting, "Eureka! Eureka!" (which means "I've found it! I've found it!"). He'd just worked out **Archimedes' principle,** which states that when a naked body is immersed in water, it experiences an upthrust. Or so he claimed in court.

Archimedes was both an engineer and a mathematician, and in addition to designing pumps and screws, he did a lot of work in mathematics and would have discovered calculus 2000 years before Newton did, if only algebra had been invented. He didn't think much of engineering, however, and much preferred the theoretical purity of mathematics, setting the pattern for mathematicians to come. He was concerned with higher things, meaningful things, like calculating the number of grains of sand in the universe; the answer he got was one, followed by 53 zeros. On many a night, Archimedes' wife could be heard shouting, "Come back to bed, Archie, no one really cares how many grains of sand there are in the universe, and besides you're making an awful mess in the living room."

The compleat bluffer always knows about the obscure as well as the famous – in fact, the more obscure the better – in order to convince even experts that you know your subject in depth. So, the next mathematician to come along is, of course, our old friend

al-Khwarizmi (*fl.* 830)

With a name like this under your belt, you can bluff your way past even a bona fide mathematician. The Romans never got around to inventing zero, so they never had scoreless ties and always played to sudden death, literally. It took many hundreds of years for this situation to be rectified. This Arab was the first to use *zero* (one of the commonest Arabic words in English after *coffee, qaddafi,* and *hashish*), from the name of the empty row in the abacus, in a major mathematical work. This was a great step forward; it meant the development of place values – thousands, hundreds, tens. (In fact, the concept of zero and place values had been developed by the Hindu mathematicians in the court of King Ashoka a couple of hundred years earlier.)

He also began to use the system of writing numerals called **Arabic numerals** – so called because it was the Arabs who first had the brilliant idea of swiping them from the Hindus. This new system outshone the old Roman numerals because never again would wiseacres insist on writing the year out as MCDMLLXXXXXIVIIVI or ask you which letter represented ten million. Incidentally, the Romans used to write 444, for example, as CCCCXXXXIIII and not CDXLIV, which was a medieval development to save paper.

Another significant advance in mathematics achieved by the Arabs (mainly, in fact, by al-Khwarizmi again) was **Kitab al-mukhtasar fi'l-hisab al-jabr wa'l-muqabalah.** When the person you're talking to asks in bewilderment what this is, feign astonishment that they've never heard of it and say, "Well, algebra, of course."

Negative numbers were probably first devised soon after by an unnamed group of Hindu economists, who immediately put their discovery to good use by inventing bounced checks. It was a long time before negative numbers were regarded as legitimate in the West, and only a siege of desperately cold Greenland-like winters in the Middle Ages convinced people that subzeros were for real. Americans, of course, have perfected its use in bankruptcy court.

The Chinese, meanwhile, despite supposedly being the most advanced civilization because they'd invented fireworks, paper, and the civil service, seem to have achieved little in mathematics. The nearest thing they had to a zero was the character meaning "nothing," which had thirteen strokes and took so long to write that it was easier just to lie and write the much quicker single stroke for "one." They thus lacked the neat Arabic system and brought up the rear in commerce, failed to export paper to the West, causing serious shortages, had no coffee trade at all, and lost the Opium War.

Galileo Galilei (1564–1642)

This Italian shocked and amazed the world when he dropped two balls from the top of the Leaning Tower of Pisa. He did this to prove that objects of different weights falling to the ground hit the earth at the same time (unsucccessful previous demonstrations involved dropping two spheres, one a pound of lead and one a pound of iron. It wasn't until many years later that the problem was discovered). If your bluffee interrogates you about *why* a ten-ton weight should drop to earth at the same speed as a feather when it clearly doesn't, mumble something about air resistance and offer to demonstrate your point by dropping a heavy object (say, their youngest child) and a light object (say, a raw egg) together from the top of the stairs. They'll suddenly accept the theory without your demonstration.

Galileo was also at the center of a ghastly misunderstanding when he was overheard talking to his wife about the earth moving. He was accused of heresy by the Catholic churchmen of the time and made to sign a confession stating that the earth did not move. Only his wife knew the real truth.

René Descartes (1596–1650)

Inventor of **Cartesian coordinates**, not wells – this Frenchman was one of the first great bluffers. "Are you sure about this?" his tutors would ask about his ideas on analytic geometry. "Well, I *think* it's true; therefore it is," he'd reply. He went on to make a lot of money out of this idea and switched to the more lucrative study of philosophy. His work reduced all geometry to just long strings of numbers, a remarkably prophetic concept in view of the fact that computers wouldn't hit the streets for over three centuries. So influential was Descartes that his model of the solar system, completely inaccurate in order to please the Catholic church, was accepted as gospel and delayed any progress in astronomy for decades.

Pierre Fermat (1601–65)

Another first-class French bluffsmith. Fermat took to mathematics only as a hobby; by profession, he was a lawyer, so he was well versed in concepts of logical argument, truth, and how to twist it. He's famous for **Fermat's last theorem,** a byword for bluffers everywhere. In a letter to a friend concerning the problem of proving that no integer solutions for n above two exist for the equation

$$a^n + b^n = c^n$$

he wrote in the margin, "I have discovered a marvelous proof of this, but the margin is not big enough to contain it."

Even today, no one has managed to prove it for all values of n, although some incredibly persistent mathematicians, with nothing better to do, have proved it for every number less than 100 except for 37, 59, and 67. No one really knows if Fermat did, indeed, have an incredibly sneaky proof which we haven't stumbled on yet or if he was just bluffing.

Kowa Seki (1642–1708)

Another mathematician so obscure that few mathematicians have even heard the name. You can look shocked at their ignorance of this Japanese who almost single-handedly and nearly from scratch discovered everything in algebra and calculus known in the West, much of it before his Occidental counterparts did. He accomplished this despite the fact that there was virtually no tradition in the subject in the East at that time and he had to devise his own notation to do so.

Given the fact that any Japanese who tried to leave the country, or any foreigner who tried to enter Japan, was executed during this period, Kowa's ability to work solo was probably fortuitous. In addition, he was a great teacher and popularizer of mathematics, and for a laugh he worked out the value of π correct to 18 decimal places, the most accurate value available at that time anywhere in the world, except for the number of syllables in a haiku.

Isaac Newton (1642–1727)

Newton's mother tried to make him drop out of school in Woolsthorpe, Lincolnshire, when he was 14 to be a farmer, but he went on to Trinity College, Cambridge, instead. During the plague, he returned home, and it was there that he saw an apple fall from a tree and from this seminal experience, by an incredible stroke of genius, worked out the laws governing the motion of every apple in the universe—a concept which he later expanded to apply to oranges, radishes, fleas, and everything else. You should, of course, know that the apple story is true and that we heard it from no less an eminence than Voltaire, who heard it from Newton's step-niece, a Mrs. Conduitt.

In the midst of all this, he invented calculus, but because he called it *fluxions,* it never took off and nothing was published. Seven years later, the German mathematician **Leibniz** rediscovered calculus but had the wisdom to call it **calculus** (after the Greek word for *pebble,* which Archimedes would have called calculus, had algebra been invented so he was able to discover it) and published his findings. He submitted his claim for the copyright to a committee of famous mathematicians, not realizing that one of them was—surprise, surprise—I. Newton. Consequently Newton's prior claim was confirmed, although Leibniz's notation was adopted. It's said that his agent wanted to give the work the rather racy title *Tropic of Calculus,* to take advantage of all the publicity, but the idea didn't fly.

The sign for integration ∫ comes from the old form of *s* used during this period, which resembled an *f*, an **integral** being, of course, a fum of a feries of fmall numbers.

Newton published his great work the *Principia Mathematica* in 1687, in which he presented the laws that control everything. You can talk knowledgeably about Newton's clockwork universe, which is, as Einstein demonstrated, a lot of malarky.

The Bernoulli Bros. of Basel — Jacques (1654-1705) and Jean (1667-1748)

This pair of wild and crazy guys invented the **calculus of variations,** totally independently but at the same time—which can be used to prove everything from the aerodynamic impossibility of a bumblebee's flight to the optimal slope of a chair lift in order to guarantee that the mechanism will smack the greatest possible number of skiers between the shoulder blades, throwing them face first into the snow. Two good words to drop into the conversation while you're talking about these two are **brachistochrone** (which sounds like a kind of dinosaur but is really a curve whose shape means you slide down in the shortest time) and **tortochrone** (a curve such that if a pendulum moved in this shape, it would keep perfect time). You certainly won't get any other chance to use them.

The B boys hated each other's guts.

Abraham de Moivre (1667-1754)

A friend of Newton's who developed the theory of mortality, annuities, and life insurance. He invented **n!**, which is used a lot in probability and gaming theory, and he worked as a consultant for gambling syndicates and insurance companies on the basis of $n!$ to finance his drinking. Living in abject poverty, he died of drink; actuaries take note.

Laplace/Legendre/Lagrange (*ca.* 1740–*ca.* 1820)

Three easily confused Frenchmen—people who spend their lives in mathematics are usually quite confused anyway. All you have to remember are the phrases **Laplace transforms, Legendre polynomials,** and **Lagrange multipliers.** If you can consistently remember which name goes with which thing, you'll be doing better than most university students.

Karl Gauss (1777–1855)

At the age of three, young Karl was correcting his father's arithmetic, and in his first lesson at school, he completed the test set by a sadistic teacher to add up all the numbers from one to 100 in one minute. He did a lot of work in all areas of mathematics, co-invented the telegraph, and was to many people the brainiest mathematician, if not the brainiest human being, ever.

William Hamilton (1805–65)

The mathematician from Dublin who invented **quaternions.** Hamilton was walking along a canal in the Irish countryside one day when he suddenly had a brainstorm:

$$i^2 = j^2 = k^2 = ijk = -1$$

So pleased was he with this idea that he scratched it on the nearest bridge, where it remains to this day. This

is a particularly beautiful piece of mathematics. No one
has ever really found a good use for it, but it looks very
nice on paper, if a little incongruous on stone bridges.

As a calculated bluffer, you'll know that Hamilton
invented Lagrangian mechanics, of course, and Lagrange invented Hamilitonian mechanics.

Hamilton spoke more then ten languages and was
an alcoholic in six of them.

Évariste Galois (1811–32)

One of the most interesting mathematicians ever. He
was jailed for antiroyalist activities in the French
revolution in 1831 and was killed in a duel at the age
of 20, having written down everything he knew the
night before so it wouldn't be lost to the world. He
didn't finish writing until dawn and was so tired he
couldn't shoot straight. Galois did a lot of work in
algebra and that kind of thing and had the brilliant idea
of just making up fictitious numbers to supply answers
to problems that didn't otherwise have a solution – an
inspired bluffing device. Simply knowing that he invented **Galois' theory** ("which is very hard to understand") will be enough for all practical purposes.

Gottlob Frege (1848–1925)

Undoubtedly the unluckiest mathematician in the
world, and not just because his father couldn't spell.
He had just received the galley proofs of *Grundgesetze
der Arithmetik*, his life's work, in 1903 when he got a
letter from Bertrand Russell, who noted that, due to

a mistake in the initial structures Frege had set up to try to describe all of mathematics completely and logically, there was a paradox (now called **Russell's paradox**), and the entire book, and Frege's life's work, was therefore completely wrong. Undeterred, Frege went gamely ahead and published the book with a note in the back to the effect that, while the entire work was wrong, he hoped people would find it interesting anyway.

William Gosset (1876–1937)

You should know that the foundation for much of statistics—the theory of errors, sampling, and so forth—was laid by this man, who worked for Guinness in Dublin and published his work under the pen name "Student," because in those days, being a student actually had more street credibility than working in a brewery.

Bertrand Russell (1872–1970)

English mathematician and philosopher who's remembered by serious mathematicians for having written *Principia Mathematica* (Russell obviously had no qualms about heisting a good title when he found one—see *Isaac Newton*) in 1910, along with Alfred North Whitehead, in which they managed to make mathematics logical (which it hadn't been up till then, one presumes). Among his lesser-known works is *In Praise of Idleness*. In 1950, he won the Nobel Prize for literature—an extraordinary feat for a mathematician.

Albert Einstein (1879-1955)

Einstein didn't talk at all till the age of three, didn't speak well until he was nine, got expelled from his school in 1894 for being "disruptive," hated exams, got into the Swiss Institute of Technology only on his second try, was a failure there, and eventually became a technical clerk (third class) in the Swiss Patent Office, where he started his famous work on relativity. If you know this, it'll impress people much more than your being able to explain the Lorentz transformation, derive $E=mc^2$, or work out the speed of light. It also provides plenty of encouragement to parents and to anyone who hates exams.

Einstein was persuaded to help in atom bomb research, much to his later regret. He was awarded the Nobel Prize in 1921 for his work on quantum theory and was offered the premiership of Israel in 1952, but refused.

He spent the last 30 years of his life being a pacifist and trying to work out **unified field theory** — one equation which describes everything in the universe — but he never quite managed it.

The story goes that Einstein's brain is still preserved in a jar somewhere in a university cupboard in California. It's never shown up on the market for sale, so its value can't be determined, but it probably wouldn't sell for as much as the average mathematics undergraduate's brain, which, of course, has hardly been used.

Kurt Goedel (1906-78)

An Austrian who depressed everyone in the trade

by showing in 1930 that there's no way of actually proving mathematics isn't just a pack of lies.

Tom Lehrer (1928–)

The only mathematician in the history of the world with a sense of humor. Best known for his satirical songs, many of which have mathematical connotations, such as "New Math."

MATHEMATICAL EDUCATION

There is, of course, a dearth of good mathematics teachers—no wonder; anyone smart enough to understand compound interest and applied statistics will be off applying his or her knowledge at HUD or an S&L and making money out of it. Why subject themselves to a lifetime surrounded by a pandemonium of punk rockers screaming across the room to each other in a classroom for 15 grand a year, they say, when they can do exactly the same thing on the floor of the New York Stock Exchange for 150.

Consequently, you'll find teachers of reading, geography, and phys ed struggling with multiplication tables and supposedly interactive, totally incomprehensible *Mr. Math Wizard* computer programs when they haven't been able to balance their checkbooks since 1975.

All of which means that in the elementary grades, a child is increasingly likely to be taught mathematics by a nonmathematician. This is a terrific development, since it means it's that much easier to bluff your way past most teachers all the way through college—and from there to a top-ten brokerage house.

Elementary School

Mathematics is fun and games in elementary school. Children cut out circles, and squares, and rectangles, add with little blocks of wood, run around the classroom pretending to be decimal points, etc. Bluffing here is straightforward. Few teachers can spot the five- or seven-sided hexagon in the middle of this chaos. And the tendency to write numbers upside down can make 2 and 5, 4 and 9, 1 and 7, and 3 and 8 interchangeable. Very useful for doubling the possibilities of the answer you write down.

High School

High school mathematics teachers are allowed to pursue their chosen careers only after they have demonstrated that their handwriting is less legible than a doctor's. At that point, they are required to complete courses in breakneck erasing — learning to erase computations a split second before students can copy them from the blackboard. Some become so proficient at this skill that they work ambidexterously, writing with one hand while erasing with the other.

A lot of mathematics teaching is still done by the ancient chalk-and-blackboard method. There are two types of blackboard to go with the two types of mathematics teacher — the old style, which is fixed and rigid and never moves an inch, and the new style, which flip-flops. Neither fulfills the simple role of providing legible information, and the canny student can sit at the rear of the room where he or she can blame all mistakes on not being able to see the board.

In high school, books become very important. It's an interesting feature of mathematics books that the titles imply that the subject gets easier as you go along. While the sixteen-year-olds are using *Advanced Algebra,* the seventeen-year-olds have *Simple Higher Algebra,* and the eighteen-year-olds are on *Algebra: Some Elementary Perspectives on Group Theory.*

The most important book to have, of course, is the answer book. If you live in a big enough city, you can haunt a used-textbook store, until you come up with the teacher's manual for your text. Voila! All the answers are yours! If you're really lucky, the answer book not only will include the answer, but also will show the teacher how the problem was solved. But in either case, the "black and white" nature of mathematics comes to the bluffer's aid. If the answers to your homework are all correct, it's impossible to prove that you didn't reach them legitimately.

There will be times, of course, when devious teachers give you problems that aren't in any book. The technique here is to have a table of random answers ready, such as

(1) $\sqrt{3/2}$
(2) $60°$
(3) ± 1
(4) $2x$

As long as the overall appearance of the answers is plausible, few teachers will be concentrating enough as they watch *Monday Night Football* or *L.A. Law* to notice that none of the answers corresponds with a question. Even if they do spot a wrong answer, it'll look reasonable enough to "show you're thinking."

If you're in doubt, draw a picture. It's well known

that individuals' perceptions of the world can be very different, so it's difficult to say someone's drawing of the path taken by a man X crossing a river R from points A to B is wrong. Pass it off as an interpretation. You can prove anything with a picture, and probably will. Certainly, a small diagram, preferably upside down, labeled with large, crisscrossing arrows on the page after the relevant problem and crammed into one corner of the margin, will impress instructors no end. So long as you appear to be visualizing the situation in your mind's eye, however idiosyncratically, you'll get the benefit of any doubt – and mathematics instructors are always in doubt.

University

There's a plethora of mathematics areas available that you can choose from in college: pure mathematics, applied mathematics, pure and applied mathematics, pure mathematics with statistics, etc., etc. For the first time, the subject splits into two sections:

Pure Mathematics

The goal of pure mathematics is to get beautiful results on paper by ignoring real life; the shorter and more compact the result, the better. Hence, pure mathematicians tend to look down on applied mathematics, with its three-foot-long equations trying to describe the movement of water down a shower drain, as a groveling and unwieldy subject getting dangerously close to engineering. The purists drink wine, play chess, listen to Bach, and put pictures by Maurits Escher on their study walls.

Applied Mathematics

This branch aims to produce models describing how things work and, by trying to describe systems more and more accurately, produces longer and longer equations that frequently ooze over several pages. Applied mathematicians look down on pure mathematicians as ivory-tower dreamers. They drink beer, play pool, listen to the Grateful Dead, and put girlie calendars on their study walls.

You're expected to prove things at this level, and so the sure-fire method of drawing pictures won't cut it, even for men crossing rivers. You can still use random answers, but tailor them to the course image. So your typical answers might now be

(1) e

(2) π

(3) ∞

(4) x^n

. . . where numbers have largely been replaced by letters.

Coping also becomes more difficult, since you're expected to provide not only the answer but also the process of arriving at that answer. So, in order to get maximum credit for working out the problems, you should include as many techniques as possible in your method. Refer to any or all of the following and you're bound to be on the right track somewhere.

Proof by Induction

A very important and powerful mathematical tool because it works by assuming something is true and then goes on to prove that therefore it *is* true. Not surprisingly, you can prove almost anything by induction—so long as the proof includes the following phrases:

- Assume true for n; then also true for $n+1$, because (followed by some plausible but messy scrawls in which n and $n+1$ appear prominently).
- But is true for $n=0$ (a few more chicken scratches with lots of zeros deposited at random through the proof).
- So is true for all n Q.E.D.

Take Logs (Please)

Broadly speaking, any equation that looks difficult will look much easier when you take logs on both sides. Taking logs on one side only is tempting for many equations, but someone might notice it.

$sin^2 + cos^2 = 1$

You can say this any time during a proof, and it'll always be relevant. In fact, this is just the Pythagorean theorem $(a^2 + b^2 = c^2)$ written in a more impressive way. Since it's the first and most favorite of all theorems, you get bonus points just for sentimental value.

Reductio ad Absurdum

By assuming something is false and showing this leads to a contradiction, you can assume it must have actually been true in the first place. This method of proof is called *reductio ad absurdum*. In practice, it means that whenever a contradiction (for "contradiction" read "screwup") arises anywhere, you need only write "reductio ad absurdum, hence the proof holds."

At the end of a proof, you write Q.E.D., which stands

not for *quod erat demonstrandum*, as the books would have you believe, but for Quite Easily Done. After a diagram you've drawn to prove something by actually constructing it, you write Q.E.F., which stands similarly not for *quod erat faciendum,* but for Quite Easily Faked.

Exams

Upper-level exams are the easiest to bluff your way through because they rest on the excellent principle that the best way of solving a problem is the most economical, a procedure usually promoted by mathematicians who can't be bothered to slog through the standard, long-winded methods — often summed up as "a lazy mathematician is a good mathematician."

You can use this to your advantage by being as lazy as possible in your exam answers. They should be of minimum length and include phrases like

- by symmetry, we can show that . . .
- it is obvious that . . .
- intuitively, we can see that . . .
- by continuity, we know that . . .
- using the associative property, we can see that . . .
- adding to infinity, we get . . .
- taking logs, differentiating, squaring both sides, rearranging, solving, integrating, and taking roots, then we have . . .

and so forth, with the answer appearing like magic in the shortest possible time. Here your table of random answers will look like

- Yes, but this is more than the number of grains of sand in the universe.

- Never.
- The answer is imaginary.
- The answer is irrational.
- The answer is irrational and imaginary.
- Solutions to this are all trivial.
- Solutions to this are all nontrivial.
- Solutions to this exist only in nine dimensions/complex numbers/your own warped imagination, etc.

Note that not only all *numbers,* but also all *symbols* have disappeared completely.

Grad Types

You'll be expected to be something of a professional mathematician in grad school, and you should choose your image accordingly. There are three, sharply defined groups of university mathematicians, which we will number 0, 1, and ∞. (The numbers 2 and 3 don't, of course, exist in high-level mathematics.)

Type 0

You're either very short or very tall with greasy hair. The only evidence for your existence is a huge list of books checked out of the library in your name and a stream of Bach playing in your room on a Sunday morning. You never, ever indulge in any sport more strenuous than solving one of Rubik's puzzles; though you may well keep score for the university's intramural flag football teams and know all the team members' stats to four decimal places. You'll probably go on for a Ph.D., but you aren't quite sure why. You've never

had a girlfriend or boyfriend. You hate drunken social-
izing in the company of people with whom you have
nothing in common, but after you graduate you'll
become either a professor or an accountant.

Type 1

The vast majority of mathematicians are type 1. You
wear steel-framed glasses, read the *Hitch Hiker's Guide
to the Galaxy*, and occasionally buy a new pair of jeans.
You like mainstream rock and heavy metal and drink
too much at parties. Your boy/girlfriend is also a
mathematician, and you don't like admitting that you
can't solve *any* of Rubik's puzzles. You put "I have a
sense of humor" on your vita sheet. If male, your name
is Fred, Ralph, or Walt. You can't be bothered to read
any further than B in the career manuals, so after
graduating, you become an accountant, an actuary, a
banker, or a barber.

Type ∞

A tiny fraction of mathematicians are the infinitely
unpredictable class. You chose mathematics because
you don't have to do essays, because you can't write.
You're quick to point out that mathematics, therefore,
of all subjects, takes the least time to do per week
because you can "either do it or you can't."

Genuine type infinity mathematicians are never, ever
seen on campus, but they're on the cross-country and
golf teams, have lost count of their girlfriends and
boyfriends, none of whom have anything to do with
mathematics, are quite proud to tell you they neither
know nor care who Rubik is, and after graduating

become absolutely anything *except* an accountant, an actuary, or a banker.

Having chosen your character, you can then proceed to bluff your way through the remainder of your education as follows.

Constructing Solutions

Occasionally, worst may come to worst and you can't find the solution anywhere. In this ominous turn of events, rely on one of these tried-and-true techniques for making incoherent answers look plausible.

Page-Turning Method

An old favorite that can keep saving your skin right up to finals. Suppose you know what you have to prove, and also how to start, but you can't get the twain to meet no matter how you sweat. All you have to do is work back as far as you can from the answer and down as far as you can from the question, engineering your pages so that the break in your reasoning coincides with the page break. You can enhance the effect by making sure this break takes you from page two, say, to halfway down page nine, thus spreading the gap across ten minutes of searching time and rendering it almost imperceptible.

Change of Variables Method

Interesting historically because it carries echoes of those halcyon days in elementary school when your amorphous handwriting could turn 2's into 5's and so forth. Here you have a staggering range of letters to choose for use in your proofs—a to z, α to ω, even Cyrillic Ж and И and Я, or Hebrew characters if you prefer. So you've got infinite scope for prestidigitation, changing one symbol into another if the need arises in the middle of a proof. The skillful bluffer can perform wonders of transformation here, changing an x to a χ, and α to δ via 0, and b to β by way of 8 and S. In this way, you can not only change one thing into another, but by judicious canceling, also get rid of unwanted letters completely or introduce totally new ones if you prefer. This is a powerful mathematical tool for the calculating conjurer or the conjuring calculator, with many applications in wide-ranging areas of the subject.

MacDonald's Lemma

Lemmas are "minitheorems," proved before a really big theorem as a sort of tool to use later. They shouldn't be confused with the suicidal furry mammals called lemmings, which are about as useful in mathematics as a lemma is in real life. All you need to know about lemmas is that **Burnside's lemma** has absolutely nothing to do with Burnside. If you're in a confident mood, you can even assert that it isn't actually a lemma either, just as you won't find a mountain oyster at any higher elevation than the pasture and you certainly won't find a pearl in it.

There's never been a mathematician of any renown by the name of MacDonald, so it's a standard choice of name to use for a lemma or theorem that you need but which doesn't exist. For example, if during the course of your solution, your proof requires that "All deformed hypernodules have an infinitely warped sub nodule" (which may or not be true and about which you neither know nor care), you merely state at the appropriate point in your exposition

"Now, by MacDonald's lemma, we know that all deformed hypernodules have a subnodule which is infinitely warped. Hence, . . ."—and away you go.

MacDonald's lemma, or theorem, is very useful, but don't overuse it. Don't use it twice on the same page to say different things, for example.

You could try, as a variation, the corollary of Mac-Donald's theorem. A corollary is a spasmodic fit under whose influence a mathematician suddenly decides to apply a theorem backwards.

Proof by Assumption

Another powerful technique. Assume that the result you want is true, and go on to prove that, if this is the case, then the proposition you're trying to prove holds, which proves the original assumption, that is, the result you want is true. Thus the problem's solved. (Politicians have recently called such a proof supply-side economics.)

Don't underestimate this one; many of the great mathematicians in history have used it more often than is generally admitted. It requires a little thought and careful wording, but the line of reasoning can usually be made tortuous enough to snow even the most attentive instructor as he or she sits in the tavern/concert/kitchen at a party grading your test paper.

Giving Wrong Answers

Rather than sit and look confused and say "I don't know," the smart bluffer will appear to get a flash of inspiration when asked a question he or she doesn't understand in the slightest and give a random answer confidently. The great thing is that mathematics can be so complex at this level that very often the difference between a procedure that eventually results in the answer and one that results in a random letter of the Cyrillic alphabet can be minimal. A good professor will try desperately to reconstruct from your answer the thought processes you must have followed, even though they're nonexistent, which can consume at least an hour of prime grading time.

Asking the Not Quite Totally Irrelevant Question

Most professors love talking, and they'll be happy to answer any questions you might have – the art is to ask questions not *actually* irrelevant to the subject of study, but those that don't require that you know a thing about them in order to discuss them. As examples try

(1) I see the man behind this theorem came from Norway (Ulan Bator, Poughkeepsie, etc.) . . . is there a tradition of mathematics there?
(2) Could this theorem have been discovered with Euclidean geometry?
(3) Is it possible to prove this using a computer?
(4) Could you work this problem using matrices?

Topics for Discussion

Mathematicians are a pretty boring bunch on the whole, and they find it difficult to talk about anything nonmathematical. Use this to your advantage. If anyone asks you what university mathematics "is like," your first line of defense is to claim that it's all awfully dry and dusty and uninteresting to the layman and difficult to understand even for the expert, so you won't bore them by talking about it. If you're pushed, however, you can claim to have studied the following:

Chaos

No one has ever satisfactorily defined chaos, but it sounds fascinating, even if it's probably unimportant. It's a new area in mathematics, so always describe it as exciting.

Fourier Series

Almost anything is, or can be, a Fourier series. They aren't very interesting, but they're very important.

Differential Equations

Differential equations rear their little heads everywhere and are, of course, very, very important and quite interesting. They're usually pretty tricky to solve but not as tricky as partial differential equations. There's only one interesting application of differential equations — working out the fluctuations in numbers of sharks breeding at a certain rate who eat fish at such and such a rate who breed at so and so speed. Exotic variations exist with populations of cockroaches, spiders, lemmings, etc.

Vector Space

There's plenty of vector space in mathematics, and it comes in all shapes and sizes – from points to sheets up to three, four, or any number of dimensions. However, few blackboards can handle four-dimensional space, so it tends to be neglected. Vector space is very important and very interesting, but not as interesting as Hilbert space, which is sometimes sold in jars to gullible tourists, just as unscrupulous locals sell stuffed jackalopes or casts of abominable snowman footprints. Hilbert space is, of course, simply a vector space in which every Cauchy sequence converges. State this with a straight face and it's guaranteed to put down almost anyone who dares challenge you.

Set Theory

Set theory is not only very interesting but also incredibly important because it's the foundation for everything in mathematics. You can prove, for example, the existence of numbers, which is useful, and even show that one and one makes two. It usually takes at least until the third year of an undergraduate course to accomplish this feat. You'll of course know Russell's paradox ("Is the set of all sets which are not members of themselves a member of itself?"– learn this by heart and you can destroy a conversation at fifty paces), which for awhile looked dangerously as though it would prove that all mathematics was false. Fortunately, the rules of set theory were redesigned to circumvent this disaster, and the world can sleep safe in the knowledge that numbers probably do exist after all.

Probability

Problems in probability are always set in infinite parking garages in which there's a drunk taking a random walk or with an infinite number of monkeys at an infinite number of typewriters. The odds of their typing an Academy Award acceptance speech are three to one (or one to three) depending on the monkeys' words per minute. It's very interesting and extremely important for people trying to remember where in the nightclub lot they left their car or what they're going to say to thank the "little people." Don't fail to mention the standard probability problem that *everyone* thinks they can answer. "What is the probability that a dime tossed once will land tails up?" "One in two, of course," your bluffee will say disdainfully. "Not so," you retort, and you proceed to explain that there is a chance, however small, that the coin will land on its edge, that a passing pigeon will eat it and it won't come down at all, etc., etc. Jimmy the Greek is perhaps the best-known modern expert in this area of mathematics.

Fluid Mechanics

Good terms here (all clearly very important and extremely interesting) are

bifurcation–The phenomenon of smoke rising up straight and then for no apparent reason wiggling out into little ripples. "The mathematics is very complex," you say, implying that you actually understand it when, in fact, no one does.

Coriolis force–The force that makes bathwater go clockwise down the drain in the northern hemisphere–or is it the south?–nobody can remember–

as a consequence of the earth's spinning, except that it isn't, because the shape of the bathtub makes all the difference.

matched wave asymptotics – "For use in harnessing wave power in the U.K.," you say, "but its big use in the U.S. is in military combat." While it's not entirely true, it sounds plausible.

Solid Mechanics

Be disparaging about solid mechanics. It's neither interesting nor important. Say it's just a heap of vibrating plates and dismiss it contemptuously as being mere engineering ("and look what happened to the San Francisco Bay Bridge," you can declare). Remember, a mathematician holds an engineer in roughly the same esteem as a lemming; both jump to unfortunate conclusions.

MATHEMATICS IN
REAL LIFE

Opportunities abound for the bluffer to display his or her knowledge of the mathematics behind the real world. Mathematicians themselves suffer from a firm belief that their subject is obscure and inaccessible and has no relevance to real life. True though this undoubtedly is in general, there are still many occasions when you can refer to some mathematical idea or reel off a couple of meaty technical terms and bring the subject alive (but note with caution that the last person to bring a subject alive was Dr. Frankenstein).

You can claim that *anything* is just simple mathematics: card tricks, hockey, running a business, playing chess, deciding in which order to do your tasks for the day, etc. The whole theory collapses, of course, because mathematicians are invariably hopeless at all of these activities (except chess — which has nothing to do with everyday life), but it's a good line to take and one that's impossible to disprove. Even behind flower arranging, or playing spin the bottle, or training gerbils to ride unicycles, there must be some beautiful mathematical principles — those no one's bothered to discover, since they've managed quite nicely without them until now.

People generally have a low opinion of mathematics and especially of mathematicians, regarding them as a peculiar breed with steel-rimmed glasses, chewed fingernails, half-zipped trousers (men and women), and an appallingly bad sense of humor. The stereotype is undoubtedly unfair – at least a few wear contact lenses. But the subject's inaccessibility is exacerbated by the fact that it appears to be so humorless. Very rare indeed is the mathematician who could be called a wit, and unfortunately, two half-wits don't make a whole wit.

Here's just one example of the nonarithmetic nature of everyday life – two halves don't always make a whole. If they always did, it would be possible to get two and a half brothers, for example, by combining one brother and three half-brothers. Often, of course, the whole is more than the sum of its parts (despite conclusive proofs to the contrary by set theoreticians in the nineteenth century), such as in a restaurant when everyone's paid their share and it still doesn't equal the total on the check. And everyone knows that two wrongs don't make a right – even though they should, the composition of two negatives being positive, of course.

For the bluffer it's essential to identify the situations where mathematics fails, and to know the rule that's being disobeyed, thereby giving the impression that you're not only practical and in touch with the world, but also that you know the deep and meaningful principles behind it, which ought to be being followed.

Proportionality

One of the most common mathematical rules that's flagrantly disobeyed in everyday life is proportionality – the idea that, if it takes one man one week to dig a trench 12 feet long, it will take seven men just one day to dig the same trench. This, of course, doesn't hold in real life; seven men will take at least three times as long as one man would, depending on their union affiliations, the number of games of gin rummy they play, and whether they're working under a government contract.

Similarly, if it takes one bureaucrat 20 minutes to find your records, you can be sure it will take five of them three hours. There's even a well-defined function for this phenomenon $N_t(p)$, the number of people needed such that if they all look for p of your records they'll lose them in t minutes. This function is of vital importance in deciding staffing levels in the civil service.

At the innumerable points on the interstate where two lanes are closed for vital purposes such as parking unused backhoes, stacking orange plastic traffic cones, determining whether two men can make a cup of coffee twice as fast as one, etc., the traffic funnels into that one remaining lane. Classical mechanics predicts that the speed of traffic flow should therefore increase threefold through that lane, which doesn't quite explain why a 20-mile backup forms immediately and everything slows to a crawl (an event generally referred to as the *gawk paradox*).

There are occasions where proportionality does hold contrary to mathematical prediction. For example, a four-piece jazz band and an eight-piece jazz band playing the same tune should take the same time, as any schoolchild could tell you, but in reality, the eight-piece group will take twice as long in order to let everyone have a solo.

Probability

Probability predicts many surprising things, none of which ever happens in real life, as you might expect. For example, the chance of getting a telephone call while you're in the shower is statistically extremely small, but empirical evidence shows this occurrence to be nearly inevitable. The chances of finding someone who knows the street you're trying to find in a strange town should be pretty high, but for some unfathomable reason, the only people you ever meet are Japanese tourists, imbeciles, and people who just moved there yesterday.

Horseracing provides many examples of the flouting of the rules of probability. For a start, as you'll point out whenever possible, odds are always stated backwards—"three to one" really mean "one in three," or a third. Also, if you add up the odds on all the horses, the total should, of course, be one because it's 100 percent certain that the race will be won by a horse. The fact that it never does total one shows how clever the bookies are at using mathematics creatively, siphoning off this discrepancy to buy BMWs, houses in Malibu, and vacations in Saint-Moritz. Very few of them ever majored in number theory.

You'll find a very dubious application of probability in life expectancy. When you're born, you have a life expectancy of 74 or whatever. But on reaching 74 as expected, you find that your life expectancy's now 86, and you can expect to live another 12 years. Similarly, on reaching 86, you find you can expect to make it to 94, and so forth. As the octogenarian said, "If they'd told me to begin with that my body was going to last this long, I'd have taken better care of it."

Weather forecasts give the chance of precipitation for the coming day — 10 percent, 80 percent, etc. You can challenge people to say exactly what "80 percent chance of precipitation" actually means. You can tell them, with a knowing smile, that it means in 80 percent of places, there will very probably be rain.

Give the impression that you understand the above two examples, but deliberately present them in a misleading way; if you can do this, you can get anyone else at a party worried that they can't figure out exactly what it all means, which will almost certainly be the case — unless, of course, they're an actuary, in which case they're not going to be invited to any good parties anyway, in all probability

Statistics

The first problem with statistics is that they're often misinterpreted. If 30 percent of all accidents are caused by drunk drivers, it means that 70 percent are caused by sober drivers, who are therefore clearly the greater danger. So you have to think about what the figures really mean, which nobody ever does, especially politicians. If a politician claims that we had the biggest industrial growth of any of the major industrialized nations in the last six months, it probably means

(1) They've all grown so much they don't need to grow much faster.

(2) Until six months ago, we were stagnating, so our
     growth rate is impressive because we started out
     in such lousy shape.

Similarly, "the rate of inflation is coming down" still
means prices are increasing and tells you little except
that the rate is probably still too high and they're not
going to tell you what it is.

Watch out for doctored graphs like those showing
the "dramatic" fall in the unemployment figures from
3,200,000 to 3,100,000, where the scale of people
unemployed on the left of the graph starts at 3,000,000,
thus making it look like the number's been cut in half.
If the graph started as it should, at zero, the effect
would be no more than a tiny shift, unidentifiable to
the naked eye, but it wouldn't be nearly so impressive.
This kind of bald-faced con happens all over the place
and scores good points for the bluffer who points it
out – if you ever see a graph with a scale not starting
at zero, you can confidently conclude that it's flimflam.

Average

You should know that the three types of commonly
used averages are the **mean,** the **median,** and the
mode. The mean is the average (add up everything and
divide by the number of things), the median is the middle term of the bunch if they're arranged in order, and
the mode is the one that appears most often. So the
"average pay" in the U.S. could be quite different depending on which kind is used – the mean (which includes the stockbrokers, and baseball players, and
robber barons) will produce a high figure (so it's usually

the one quoted by the government to show us how *well* we're doing), the mode will produce a low figure (because most people earn a low salary – so it's quoted by the outs). The mean can often give misleading impressions – for example, while the mean number of children in the U.S. is 1.8 per family, or whatever, the mode is 2. Always question a figure if it's quoted as an "average" – "*Which* average? It makes a big difference, doesn't it?" – etc. Whichever one it is, insist that it should be one of the others.

Mathematical Increases

Anything that gets bigger faster than you expect is called a **geometric progression.** Something that gets bigger faster than you'd expect and goes *on* getting bigger faster and faster is an **exponential increase,** although you never get those in real life. Even the combined national debts of South America aren't increasing *quite* exponentially.

Be sure to say something impressive whenever people complain about credit-card payments – "Yes, they deliberately mislead you because they quote you monthly rates, which are geometric means," that kind of thing.

Population is something else that tends to increase faster than you'd expect. By the year 2000, the world will no longer be able to be packed shoulder-to-shoulder in Vermont, and every other person will be either a Chinese or an Arab, a situation already true in many cities. Environmentally aware types will know that the ability of the earth to sustain life increases only **arithmetically** (that is, about as quick as you'd expect), whereas the number of mouths to feed increases **geometrically,** "and I don't have to tell you what *that* means," you can say ominously.

Another equally ominous example of a geometric increase is the number of patients with some highly infectious disease. Start with one carrier, let him or her make five contacts, and so forth. Working out whether – by combining the twin effects of population increase through lack of birth control and decrease through death by disease – the overall figure will go up or down calls for **differential equations,** and by this time you'll have scared everyone sufficiently to keep them from asking you what a differential equation is.

Geometry

By knowing the names of the various shapes you encounter, you'll give the impression of being someone who knows and understands how things tick. Bluffers should know that the cables on suspension bridges, pulled down by the weight of the box sections, assume the form of **parabolas,** which, you will continue confidently, is the same shape as the reflectors in car headlights and electric heaters, as if the connection were obvious. In fact, the connection is very tenuous – parabolas are used in lights because they reflect the light from the bulb into a straight beam, which clearly has nothing to do with suspension bridges at all.

However, any freely suspended ropes, cables, or strings – clotheslines, for example, after the underwear has been stolen – take the shape of **catenaries.** You'll also mention offhandedly that the equation of a catenary is really quite simple, just "e to the x plus e

to the minus x," as if you understand what you're saying, and as if anyone could tell the difference anyway.

Cooling towers at power stations are **hyperbolas** because, as you'll point out, this shape can be constructed with steel girders — difficult as it is to believe, cooling towers are made entirely of straight girders, all of which link the top and bottom at a skewed angle. Whether you can visualize it or not, make it seem as though you can, clearly and easily.

Snails' shells are **logarithmic spirals,** which have the odd property that they look the same from six inches as from a million miles away — and if the snails are in a really strong garlic sauce, a million miles is probably the safer bet.

Remember that *hyperbola* and *parabola*, being Latin words, can take either -*s* or -*e* in the plural, and whichever the other person uses, you should correct them and say it's the other one.

The **circle** has many well-known properties, such as occasionally being vicious, but it's chiefly useful because of its ability to serve as a wheel. The circumference of any circular shape, say a pie, divided by the diameter is always the same. According to the Bible, this is three. The Greeks knew it to be 3.1416, the value generally used today, and the number was called π. Since then, things have gone downhill. The Italian Vieta calculated it to ten decimal places in the 1500s, the German van Ceulen went to 35 and had them engraved on his tombstone, and recently, hours of valuable computer time have been wasted in calculating it to millions of places, when eight or thereabouts is quite accurate enough to be able to get to the moon. And for most of us just trying to get to Pittsburgh, we can take the Bible's word for it and use three.

You should know the mnemonic (cute little memory joggers which work for everything except remembering how to spell "mnemonic") in which the number of letters in each word gives π:

How I want a drink, alcoholic of course, after the heavy lectures involving quantum mechanics (3.14159265358979).

A teetotal version exists beginning "May I have a large container of coffee . . . ," and obscene variations can often be found on the restroom walls near any mathematics classroom.

Relativity

Relativity is fertile ground for bluffers because the mathematics is so incredibly complex that everyone shies away from it, but the effects and consequences are so interesting that everyone likes to discuss it in superficially convincing, "man-in-the-street" terms without really knowing anything detailed about it at all, which is exactly what the bluffer aims to do.

First, you point out that the mathematics of relativity is very, very complex, and repeat the following story. When Einstein's theories were published, the famous English physicist Eddington was asked if it was true that he was one of only three people in the world who understood it, and his silence was first taken to be a sign of modesty. In fact, Eddington was trying to think who the third person could possibly be.

Having established this, you can smilingly claim a

"rough appreciation" of some of the effects. Einstein's **Theory of Special Relativity** in 1905 concerned the effects of two observers moving relative to each other and showed that each one thinks the other's watch is slow, their rulers are too short, and they're putting on weight, but that they, themselves, are quite normal. This obviously flies in the face of reality where people who *don't* move relative to anything are usually the ones who put on weight. If your audience can stay with you that far, you can flummox them completely by stressing that all these effects are relative.

Einstein's **Theory of General Relativity** in 1916 went further and showed that gravity distorts the space-time continuum, a phrase you should use constantly if you want to sound convincing. So clocks tick slower near large gravitational sources, meaning that fat people's watches are liable to be wrong. (A particularly effective trick here is to make sure your own watch is slightly fast and challenge a weighty individual to compare times.) Time moves fractionally (but, with sophisticated instruments, measurably) slower on the lower floors of buildings, for example, because they're nearer to the earth, and especially slowly on the ground floors of office buildings between three-thirty and five o'clock on Fridays.

If some wiseacre tries to test you by hinting at the famous quotation $E=mc^2$, you should smile in a superior way and remind them that that particular equation was not big news and was pretty well known before Einstein. It was, you note, regrettably the basis of atom-bomb theory. The whole business of using mathematics to kill people is so depressing that the conversation will go no further and you can retire with your total ignorance of what $E=mc^2$ actually represents unchallenged.

Topology

Preface any comment on topology by saying that it's one of the new and interesting areas of mathematics, both these terms being extremely relative. Topology asks you to consider that everything is made of Plasticene and rubber sheets, and it sounds as if it were designed by perverts. Topologists are a downtrodden bunch and are fed up with hearing the joke that to make a rubber ball topologically equivalent to a sheet it only takes a prick.

The first topology problem was about the possibility of crossing all the bridges to an island in Königsberg in one journey without going over the same bridge twice, and from there it's progressed to the theory of coloring maps and fastening locks and tying knots, further evidence that it was designed *for* perverts as well.

A famous little topology problem is trying to link every one of three houses to each of three outhouses without the paths crossing; it's impossible.

You can mention maps as "good examples of topology" and that Greenland always looks so big and icy, cold, barren, and glacier-ridden because of the distortion encountered when you try to flatten a globe into a map (but say "represent a sphere in two dimensions"—it sounds better).

A good topological theorem to mention anytime is the theorem which, in essence, states that however you try to comb the hair on a hairy ball, you can't ever do it smoothly—the so-called "hairy-ball" theorem. (Is anyone absolutely sure that all topologists *aren't* perverts?) While discussing the "hairy-ball" theorem, you can make snide comments about the grooming of the party hosts' dog or cat as you pick the hairs off your jacket.

The Golden Ratio

A number that crops up everywhere is $(\sqrt{5}+1)/2$, or 1.618 . . . This number is the solution to various problems in mathematics, but its chief importance is that a rectangle with its sides in this ratio seems to be the most pleasing shape possible, and it can be found in architecture everywhere, except of course in modern architecture. You can impress people enormously by measuring the height and width of any pleasing rectangular shape (say, a piece of paper) and showing that when you divide one by the other you get 1.618. You can blow their minds completely by adding that, according to one survey, the ratio of a woman's height to the height of her navel above the ground is— surprise, surprise—1.618 . . .

Counting

Tenuous though the link with real mathematics is, you'll probably end up having to do some bluffing on numbers sooner or later.

The system of counting on fingers is not as universal as you might think—in Japan, it's the number of fingers you *don't* hold up that determines the number you're trying to express, and the signs for 1, 2, 3, etc.

are the same as those for 9, 8, 7, which makes you wonder how on earth the Japanese are the best mathematicians in the world by a long shot.

At the other end of the scale, there's the eternal confusion between the American system of counting with its characteristic hyperbole in which 1,000,000,000 is a billion, while in Britain it would only be a thousand million. This system continues so that, for example, a U.S. trillion is only a billion in the U.K. All these figures are never used except in Defense Department budgets where money is no object anyway (as former Secretary of Defense Caspar Weinberger reputedly said, "A billion here, a billion there – it all adds up") and in South America for buying houses, cars, stamps, etc. So if you're a politician, you can pick and choose between the systems depending on what particular brand of snake oil you're selling at the moment – using the British system for counting, say, the number of homeless on the streets of New York and the U.S. system for figuring the amount of money spent on low-cost housing.

In the Orient, people count in units of ten thousand, not thousands as in the West. So they call a million "one hundred ten-thousands." In Japan, for example, they call a millionaire a ten-thousand-aire, a fountain pen a ten-thousand-year-brush, and toast each other with "banzai," which means "ten thousand years."

In India it's even worse – they count in units of one hundred thousand and ten million in a desperate attempt to keep the population figures down.

When it comes to counting floors, Britain is also out of step with the eminently more sensible American system. The U.S. recognizes a fact that any preschooler could tell you is patently obvious. The floor you walk in on from the street is floor number one. So what do you call it? You got it – the "first" floor. You walk up one floor (1+1 right?), and you're on the second floor, no problem. The British, on the other hand, perversely call the second floor the first floor, leaving themselves with the inescapable paradox of having no choice but to call the first floor the zero floor, implying that it doesn't exist at all, when we all know perfectly well that it does.

In France there are, with characteristic Gallic non-conformism, four hundred degrees in a circle. They call them centigrades; so they get in all kinds of trouble when foreigners start talking about temperatures. Perhaps the 400-degree circle explains why the French never achieved much renown as explorers. It must have been frustrating setting sail at 380 degrees when your compass only went to 360.

Calculating

The system we learn in the West for multiplication is by no means the best. Calculating prodigies who can multiply 6483976 by 55601243 in their heads in ten seconds use a variety of shortcuts "so simple kids do them easily but adults can't," meaning that only children would be naive enough to think that being able to multiply 6483976 by 55601243 in their heads in ten seconds is a really cool thing to be able to do.

The Greeks, with their cumbersome way of writing calculations down longhand, used to do their addition by moving little stone balls around in grooves in the sand (hence, from the Greek word for stone ball, *calculus,* comes our word for not only "calculate" but also "calculus," which many people wish had *stayed* in the sand).

You can impress a lot of people by showing them an alternate way of multiplying which uses only addition and dividing by two "known to the ancients for centuries" (twaddle, of course).

Suppose you're multiplying 29 by 13. Draw two columns on a pad, or restaurant tablecloth, or the road grime on your car and put 29 at the top of the left and 13 at the top of the right. Down the 29 column, keep dividing by two and ignoring remainders ("the ancients didn't understand fractions") so you end up with a column reading 29, 14, 7, 3, 1. Then double the 13 the same number of times so you get a column reading 13, 26, 52, 104, 208. Then say that the ancients believed that even numbers in the left-hand column, along with their right-hand partners, were evil, or some such drivel, and cross out the 14 and its partner 26. Add up the remaining 13, 52, 104, and 208 and you get 377, the answer, as if by magic.

Don't try to explain why this works (and it always does), but smile smugly and say, "It's obvious once you see it." You can go even further and claim that children always think it's obvious, but adults can't see it because they've been brainwashed by education. Absolute garbage, of course—most kids would lose interest after five seconds and just start picking their noses—but it's a sure-fire way to get people worrying about the decline in their faculties.

PUZZLES AND TEASERS

There's always some fool at a party who takes pleasure in asking mindbending brainteasers. They're the kind of people who used to shout, "Your back wheel's moving" at cyclists when they were snotnosed kids. Fortunately, there are only a few of these brainteasers, and they're always asked in the same form – the answers are outlined below. You can try two approaches: either pretend you're actually working out the answer and get it in a flash of inspiration or give the answer before they've finished asking the question (or even before they've started). In practice, the latter is more impressive and gets rid of these pests faster.

The Lying Natives

You're asked to imagine the preposterous scenario of being in the jungle where there are two tribes, one which always tells the truth, the other which always lies. You come to a fork in the road and want to know which road leads to town, but you don't know which tribe the native sitting by the roadside belongs to. What question do you ask?

The usual answer – "If I asked you if this road led to the town, would you say 'yes'?" – is ridiculous, since no liars worth their salt would get taken in by such a cheap trick. The liar's aim is to deceive, and he or she won't fall for logical tricks. Instead, you could try something like "Did you know there's free beer today in town?" The truth teller will say "no" and run off down the road to town; the liar will say "yes" and run off down the road to town.

Of course, really professional liars would say "yes" and stay put, or run off down the wrong road deliberately, but you'd have the consolation of making them worry that they were missing out on the free beer.

The Barber

The barber in a certain town shaves all the people who don't shave themselves. Who shaves the barber?

This is meant to be a clever little paradox with no solution, but you can annoy the asker intensely by saying it's easy and the barber is a woman.

You can then ask the following (a version of Russell's paradox—point that out too): In a library there are some books that list themselves in their bibliographies and some that don't. A librarian prepares a new book for the catalogue section that's a list of all books that don't list themselves. Should he or she include this book in its own list? If so, then it becomes a book that lists itself, so it shouldn't be in the list of books that don't and vice versa. This should keep the most determined assailant at bay while you attack the Chivas Regal.

The Mixed Red and White Wine

There are two glasses of wine, one white and one red. A teaspoonful of wine is taken from the red and mixed in with the white. Then a teaspoonful of this mixture is taken and mixed in with the red. Which is bigger, the amount of red in the white or the amount of white in the red?

The answer is that they're both the same because there's the same volume in each glass, so whatever quantity of red is in the white must be equal to the quantity of white in the red. However, in practice, it's impossible to do this because the white always runs out first at parties and the red always gets spilled on someone's white pants.

The Wolf

If Little Red Riding Hood gets a head start to grandma's house and if the only way that the wolf can get there in time to eat granny, put on her clothes and makeup, and hop into her bed is by taking a shortcut through the Black Forest, how far can the wolf go into the forest? Only halfway, of course—after that, he's going out of the forest.

The Chess Board

An Indian pundit beat a Maharajah at chess, and for his reward, he demanded a grain of rice on the first square of the board, two on the second, four on the third, eight on the fourth, and so forth. How much rice did the Maharajah have to cough up?

The answer is $2^{64}-1$, more rice than even Uncle Sam could imagine surplusing. A similar problem asks you to say how thick a piece of paper folded 64 times is, and the answer is always "Higher than the moon," although in reality, you can't fold it more than eight times. If you don't believe us, try it.

The Shoes

Imelda Marcos has a rack filled with 50 black and 50 white shoes which, to add a touch of realism, is in a pitch-black closet. How many shoes must she grab to make sure of getting two of the same color?

The answer is three, in theory, but everyone says 51. In practice, the answer is 100 because Imelda has never been able to stop at one pair of shoes.

The Balance Scale

If, by using a balance scale and five weights, a man can weigh any item from 1 to 32 pounds (in even pounds), how many pounds does each of the weights weigh? The answer to this classic problem isn't important because you should confuse people by commenting on the ethical significance of the misuse of balance scales in contemporary society. But, be that as it may, discounting pilferage, slant of the weighing table, and wind-chill factor, the weights are 1, 2, 4, 8, and 16 pounds.

The Hotel Clerk

A hotel clerk is fixing the numbers on the hotel doors for all the rooms from one to 100. How many figure nines are required?

The answer is 20, but in practice, some nines get put

up as sixes and vice-versa, so the real figure could be anything.

The Pond

A pond doubles its size every day. On the twelfth day it stops. On what day was if half full?
The eleventh.

GLOSSARY

There are many innocent words in English, the most useful of which are listed below, which have been appropriated by mathematicians and used for their own peculiar ends (an affliction quite common among closeted academics). Sprinkle your conversation with these double-dealing words and you'll impress both the nonmathematicians (who'll think you're using the word in its mathematical sense) and the mathematicians (who'll think you're using the word in its everyday sense and making a subtle pun on the mathematical reference).

Algorithm — Not a "logarithm" but any sneaky calculating trick — clearly, because of the *al-* (*the* in Arabic), a word coined by Arabic mathematicians — al-gorithm (as in al-batross, al-chemy, al-cohol, al-gebra, and al-paca, but not in al-jolson.

Argument — What mathematicians get into when they try to solve real problems with imaginary numbers or imaginary problems with real numbers.

Asymptote — A line is referred to as the asymptote of a curve if the line and the curve get so close to each other that they become intimate but never formally meet, touch, or make a commitment. Referring to someone as an asymptote is not a compliment.

Calculator — Time-saving device for doing arithmetic,

which in particular means you can figure out what 11 times 12 is without chanting the entire 12's multiplication table. Consequently, it's considered a symptom of moral decline by the older generation.

Chaos – Exciting new area of mathematics which deals with being able to say just when something unpredictable is going to happen.

Chess – Strenuous physcial exercise for pure mathematicians.

Complex number – (a) the hybrid offspring of a real number and an imaginary number or (b) any number too difficult to remember offhand, like your telephone number or zip code.

Differentials – Infinitesimally small increases in something which actually make a big difference, as in pay differentials.

Discrete space – Pretend world in which everything is exactly the same distance from everything else, thus ensuring that everyone has equal privacy while working with differential equations.

Euler's line – "Whatcha doin' tonight, toots?" or where the orthocenter and the centroid meet.

Excluded third – The idea that everything is either true or false. The validity of this theorem is highly disputed in all political rhetoric.

Fluid mechanics – The study of the movement of fluids. Term used by college math majors for pre-finals brewski bashes.

Fundamental constructions – Simplistic, basic geometric constructions that take two seconds to draw and five hours to show the proof of why they are simplistic and basic. Drawing a line one inch long is an example.

Group theory—An exceedingly beautiful branch of pure mathematics used for showing how many different ways blocks of wood can be painted. Introduced in advanced calculus courses and often seen on *Sesame Street*.

Hyperbolic functions—Hyperbolic equivalents (shin, chos, than—not to be confused with owners of an Oriental fast-food joint) of the circular functions (sin, cos, tan) which have a vastly exaggerated and overrated importance.

Identity—Any member of a group that has no discernible effect on any of the others, like sober fans at a football game or a mathematician anywhere—zero in addition or one in multiplication.

Imaginary number—A pretend answer to an equation that otherwise wouldn't have any solutions, like the square root of minus one—so called because it's impossible to imagine what on earth it all means.

Infinitesimal calculus—Calculus dealing with numbers and limits that are so small they can't be written by the human hand or seen by the human eye.

Integration—Something that mathematicians perfected hundreds of years before the concept of a multicultural society.

Intuition—Claiming something you can't actually prove is obvious. Also the sneaking suspicion that partying until 3:00 A.M. on the night before your calculus finals would not be a good idea.

Irrational number—That terrific blond in the third row of your Trig class who won't go out with you. Also, a number which can't be expressed by any fraction, like the square root of two, and keeps appearing irrationally in problems where it's least expected.

Lemma—A condition affecting mathematics students whereby they prove things before starting on the main proof of a theorem; a student who can't remember which of two lemmas he's supposed to use is said to be in a dilemma.

Logarithms—Colloquially known as "logs" in a desperate attempt to squeeze some humor out of this tedious calculating device.

Matrix—Plural *matrices*. A set of figures arranged into rows and columns which no one understands, like an airline schedule—from the Latin word *matrix* meaning *womb*.

Natural numbers—Organically grown numbers—used especially for rating the bods on *au naturel* beaches.

Operations research—The inefficient mathematical study of efficiency in technical processes, the usual conclusion of which is that the operations researchers will have to be terminated.

Partial derivatives—Derivatives biased towards *x*, *y*, or *z* instead of treating all three equally—the sign for this is a six written backwards or a nine written upside down.

Perfect number – (See the blond in the third row under *irrational number*.) A number which is just too good to be true, like 28, or 36-24-36, or 46-32-34, depending on your point of view.

Prime number – A number at the height of its potency (see the blond in the third row) or any number with no divisors except itself and one.

Pure mathematician – Anyone who prefers set theory to sex.

Quadratic – Something with x^2's, x's, and numbers in it. If it also contains x^3, then it's cubic. If there's anything involving x^7, it's septic.

Rational number – A number you can reason with. The technical name for a fraction, so called because, if you take all the fractions there are and divide them among an infinite number of people, for reasons of your own, you can ration them out exactly.

Real number – Almost all the numbers you'd care to know, including those in the cracks between fractions like root two and π. The real numbers are dense; unlike the rationals, they can't be divided evenly among even an infinite number of irrational people, and you'd have to be really dense to try it.

Repeating decimal – A group of numbers which recurs forever and wastes forests of paper when you stupidly try to write some fractions as decimals.

Roots – Values of x which make the equation true. Like many discriminated-against and misunderstood minorities, mathematicians are always searching for their roots.

Set of all sets—Now frowned upon concept of early set theory which included in its members a crew cut, a goldfish named Chico, a stale cinnamon and raisin bagel, and half an accountant (before taxes).

Sin, cos, tan, cot, sec, cosec—Nicknames for a popular singing group of the 50s whose hit song was "My Baby's Got the Best Parabola in Town." Also formulas derived from the sides of triangles but which crop up in completely unexpected places. Sins are extremely common, but rarely do you encounter secs in mathematics (except possibly at M.I.T. on the weekends).

Solid mechanics—Branch of mathematics concerned with the behavior of solids and simple solid masses under stress and deformation, used especially to study solids such as metal containers with ring pulls and simple solid masses such as defensive linemen of Big Eight and Big Ten football teams.

Surds – Opposite *absurds*. Irrational numbers you step in.

Topology—A sadistic branch of mathematics that deals with the twisting of surfaces and in which Sylvester Stallone and Pee-wee Herman are equivalent because everything is made of rubber.

Transcendental number—A number that's not the root of any equation, like π and e, and that can be understood only after several hours' meditation in the lotus position.

Transitive relation—If Carol has a relationship with Bob and Bob has a relationship with Alice, then Carol and Alice are related.

Bluffer's Guides

CENTENNIAL PRESS

The biggest bluff about the *Bluffer's Guides* is the title. These books are full of information — and fun.

NOW IN STOCK — $3.95

Bluff Your Way in Baseball
Bluff Your Way in British Theatre
Bluff Your Way in Computers
Bluff Your Way in the Deep South
Bluff Your Way in Football
Bluff Your Way in Golf
Bluff Your Way in Gourmet Cooking
Bluff Your Way in Hollywood
Bluff Your Way in Japan

Bluff Your Way in Management
Bluff Your Way in Marketing
Bluff Your Way in Music
Bluff Your Way in New York
Bluff Your Way in the Occult
Bluff Your Way in Paris
Bluff Your Way in Public Speaking
Bluff Your Way in Wine
Bluffer's Guide to Bluffing

NEW TITLES

Bluff Your Way in the Great Outdoors
Bluff Your Way in Home Maintenance
Bluff Your Way in Math
Bluff Your Way in Office Politics
Bluff Your Way in Philosophy
Bluff Your Way in Psychology
Bluff Your Way in Sex

To order any of the Bluffer's Guides titles above,
use the order form on the next page.

AVAILABLE SOON

Bluff Your Way in Basketball
Bluff Your Way in Dining Out
Bluff Your Way in Etiquette
Bluff Your Way in Fitness
Bluff Your Way in Las Vegas
Bluff Your Way in London
Bluff Your Way in Marriage
Bluff Your Way in Parenting
Bluff Your Way in Politics
Bluff Your Way in Relationships

Get Bluffer's Guides at your bookstore or use this order form to send for the copies you want. Send it with your check or money order to:

Centennial Press
Box 82087
Lincoln, NE 68501

Title	Quantity	$3.95 Each
Total Enclosed		

Name_____

Address_____

City _____

State_____ Zip_____